If you are lucky enough to stumble upon a unicorn,
You'll be amazed by its colorful horn.

It may even be a benefit for you to ask,

The Benefits of Unicorn Earwax

To Macey, Henry
With Love, William
Brandy Noice
June 2022

Brandy Noice

illustrated by Gustyawan

May I borrow a bit of earwax?

Now, that may seem strange and quite bizarre,

But unicorn earwax is the greatest miracle cure by far!

It is a well-known fact that unicorn earwax cures the common cold.

And the secret is that it even kills stinky mold!

I even once heard a rumor.

Some say that it improves your sense of humor.

If you want to eliminate cellulite or
get rid of wrinkles,

Then apply unicorn earwax which looks like frosting with sprinkles!

Make sure that you apply it day and night.

It will keep you
looking just right!

If you are struggling in school.

A teaspoon a day is the rule.

It will help you solve the math problems that you don't know how to do.

The secret is, it even tastes yummy
and oh so sweet.

Unicorn earwax makes the best lip balm, everyone agrees!

And it keeps you from having two squeaky knees.

It is the absolute best gift
for your mother.

Oh, and do you have a pesky little brother?

WELL...

But seriously, a unicorn is the very best friend to keep.

Even if you never meet a Unicorn in real life, something magical happens when you sleep.

You may drift off to dreamland with
cotton candy clouds so sweet.

And maybe, just maybe, a unicorn you will meet.

She will have that magical earwax in her ears,
But you have to go say hi before she disappears.

So, if you ever stumble on a
unicorn while you slumber,

PLEASE, OH PLEASE, WOULD YOU GIVE THEM MY NUMBER?

Made in the USA
Monee, IL
21 June 2022